EVERYDAY ENGINEERING

Bridges

by Chris Bowman

BELLWETHER MEDIA • MINNEAPOLIS, MN

BLASTOFF! READERS

2

Note to Librarians, Teachers, and Parents:

Blastoff! Readers are carefully developed by literacy experts and combine standards-based content with developmentally appropriate text.

Level 1 provides the most support through repetition of high-frequency words, light text, predictable sentence patterns, and strong visual support.

Level 2 offers early readers a bit more challenge through varied simple sentences, increased text load, and less repetition of high-frequency words.

Level 3 advances early-fluent readers toward fluency through increased text and concept load, less reliance on visuals, longer sentences, and more literary language.

Level 4 builds reading stamina by providing more text per page, increased use of punctuation, greater variation in sentence patterns, and increasingly challenging vocabulary.

Level 5 encourages children to move from "learning to read" to "reading to learn" by providing even more text, varied writing styles, and less familiar topics.

Whichever book is right for your reader, Blastoff! Readers are the perfect books to build confidence and encourage a love of reading that will last a lifetime!

This edition first published in 2019 by Bellwether Media, Inc.

No part of this publication may be reproduced in whole or in part without written permission of the publisher. For information regarding permission, write to Bellwether Media, Inc., Attention: Permissions Department, 6012 Blue Circle Drive, Minnetonka, MN 55343.

Library of Congress Cataloging-in-Publication Data

Names: Bowman, Chris, 1990- author.
Title: Bridges / by Chris Bowman.
Description: Minneapolis, MN : Bellwether Media, Inc., [2019] | Series:
   Blastoff! Readers. Everyday Engineering | Includes bibliographical
   references and index. | Audience: Ages 5-8. | Audience: Grades K to 3.
Identifiers: LCCN 2018000203 (print) | LCCN 2018001378 (ebook) | ISBN 9781626178212
   (hardcover : alk. paper) | ISBN 9781681035628 (ebook)
Subjects: LCSH: Bridges–Juvenile literature.
Classification: LCC TG148 (ebook) | LCC TG148 .B68 2019 (print) | DDC 624.2–dc23
LC record available at https://lccn.loc.gov/2018000203

Editor: Paige V. Polinsky   Designer: Jeffrey Kollock

Printed in the United States of America, North Mankato, MN

Table of **Contents**

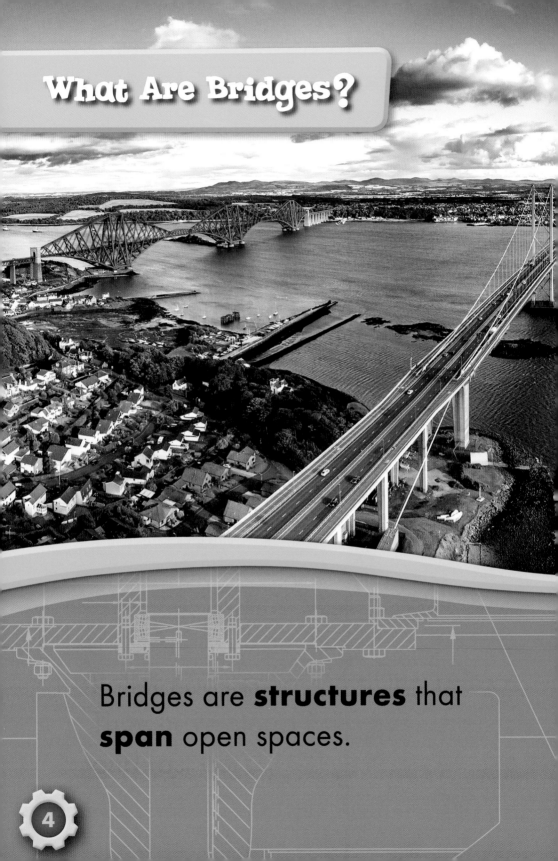

What Are Bridges?

Bridges are **structures** that **span** open spaces.

They are often built for cars
and trains. Some are made
for walking.

Many bridges are built
in cities or near water.

Others are in hilly areas. They help people cross over **obstacles**.

Early bridges were made of wood or rope. Others were stone and brick.

steel and
concrete

Today, many are built with
steel and **concrete**.
They are much stronger.

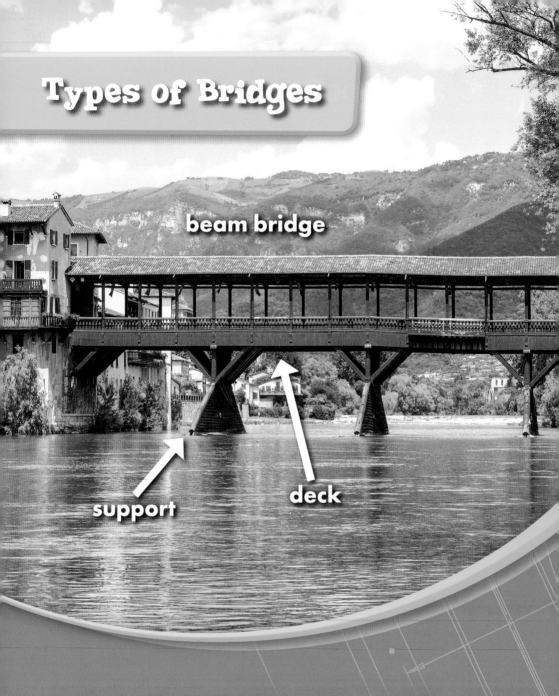

beam bridge

support

deck

Many beam bridges are short. Their flat **decks** rest on **supports**.

Arch bridges have curved frames. These often span short to medium lengths.

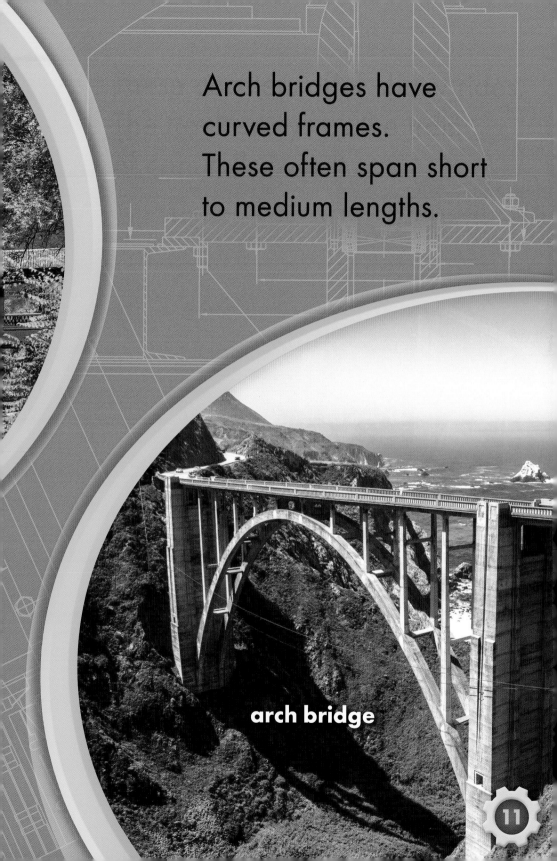

arch bridge

11

Truss bridges have frames
shaped like triangles.
They hold heavy **loads**.

truss bridge

arms

cantilever bridge

Cantilever bridges have two arms.
Each arm is held firmly at one end.
They connect in the middle.

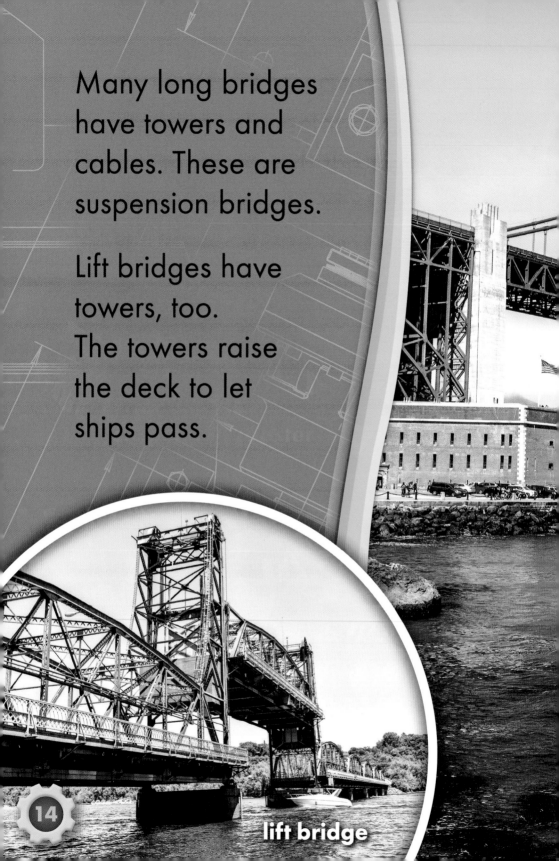

Many long bridges have towers and cables. These are suspension bridges.

Lift bridges have towers, too. The towers raise the deck to let ships pass.

lift bridge

cables

tower

Golden Gate Bridge

Location: San Francisco, California

Type: suspension bridge

Year Completed: 1937

Engineer: Joseph B. Strauss

Length:

main deck: 4,200 feet (1,280 meters)

total: 9,150 feet (2,789 meters)

How Do Bridges Work?

Bridges experience two main forces. **Compression** often acts on the top of the deck.

This can place **tension** on the rest of the bridge.

Forces at Work

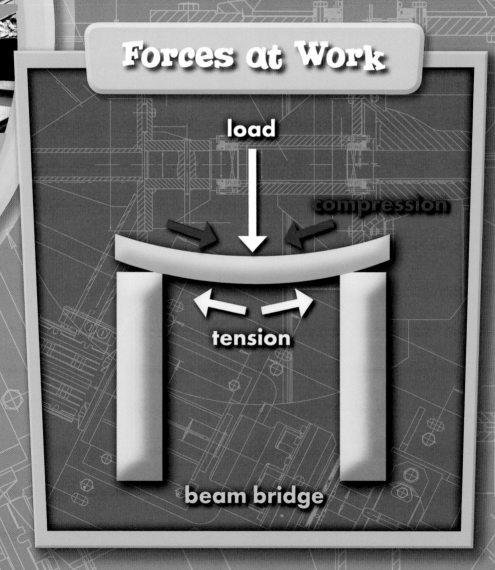

load

compression

tension

beam bridge

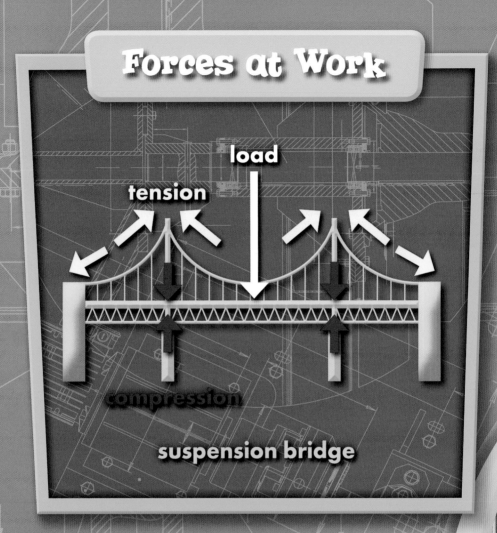

Forces at Work

load

tension

compression

suspension bridge

Frames and supports
help bridges balance
the forces from the load.

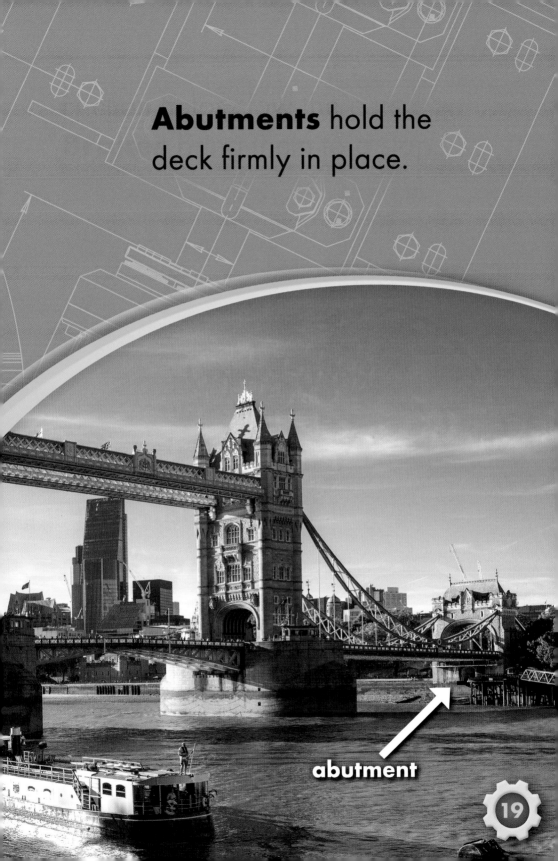

Abutments hold the deck firmly in place.

abutment

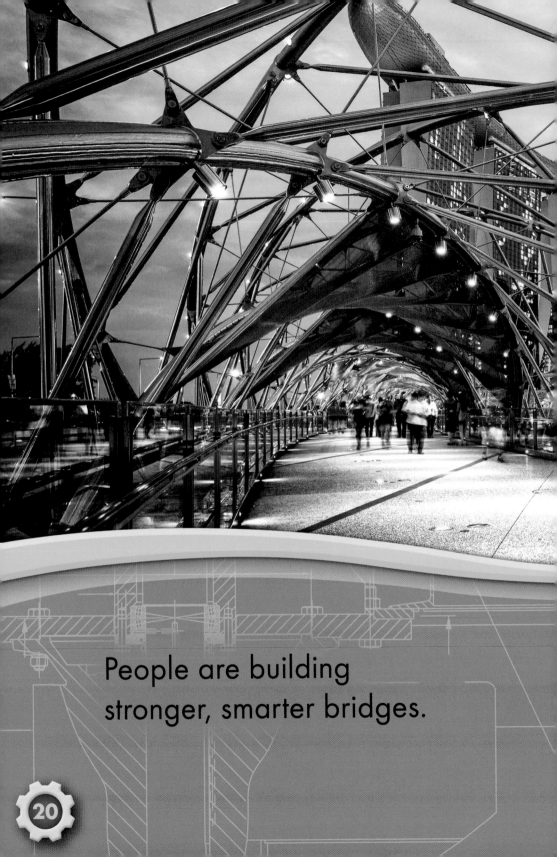

People are building
stronger, smarter bridges.

20

Some bridges send warnings
when they need to be fixed.
They help us travel safely!

Glossary

abutments—supports near the ends of a bridge deck

compression—a force that pushes inward

concrete—a hard building material made of stone, cement, and water

decks—flat parts of bridges used as roadways or walkways

loads—weights or pressures

obstacles—objects that stand in the way

span—to cross from one place to another

structures—things that are built

supports—parts that help hold up a structure

tension—a force that pulls outward

To Learn More

AT THE LIBRARY

Enz, Tammy. *Building Bridges*. Chicago, Ill.:
Heinemann Raintree, 2017.

Isbell, Hannah. *Zoom in on Bridges*. New York, N.Y.:
Enslow Publishing, 2018.

Polinsky, Paige V. *Bridges*. Minneapolis, Minn.:
Abdo Pub., 2017.

ON THE WEB

Learning more about
bridges is as easy as 1, 2, 3.

1. Go to www.factsurfer.com.

2. Enter "bridges" into the search box.

3. Click the "Surf" button and you will see a
   list of related web sites.

With factsurfer.com, finding more information is
just a click away.

Index